A+
books™

Eat Your Colors

Brown Food Fun

by Lisa Bullard

Capstone
press

Mankato, Minnesota

A+ Books are published by Capstone Press,
151 Good Counsel Drive, P.O. Box 669, Mankato, Minnesota 56002.
www.capstonepress.com

1 2 3 4 5 6 11 10 09 08 07 06

Library of Congress Cataloging-in-Publication Data
Bullard, Lisa.
    Brown food fun / by Lisa Bullard.
    p. cm.—(A+ books. Eat your colors)
    Includes bibliographical references and index.
    ISBN-13: 978-0-7368-5380-4 (hardcover)
    ISBN-10: 0-7368-5380-4 (hardcover)
    1. Food—Juvenile literature. 2. Brown—Juvenile literature. I. Title. II. Series.
TX355.B922 2006
641.3–dc22   2005026669

Summary: Brief text and colorful photos describe common foods that are the color brown.

Credits
Donald Lemke, editor; Kia Adams, designer; Kelly Garvin, photo researcher

Photo Credits
Capstone Press/Karon Dubke, all

Note to Parents, Teachers, and Librarians
This Eat Your Colors book uses full-color photographs and a nonfiction format to introduce
children to the color brown. *Brown Food Fun* is designed to be read aloud to a pre-reader or to be
read independently by an early reader. Photographs help listeners and early readers understand
the text and concepts discussed. The book encourages further learning by including the following
sections: Recipe, Glossary, Read More, Internet Sites, and Index. Early readers may need assistance
using these features.

Table of Contents

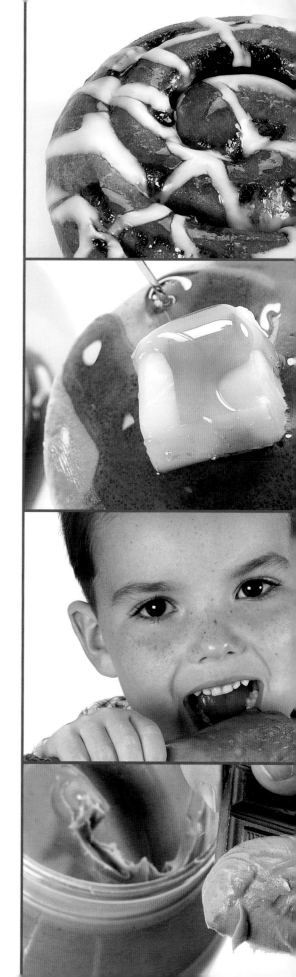

Delicious Brown

Smooth or creamy, saucy or crunchy, brown foods can be a bit nutty. What brown food is your favorite?

Crack! The walnut's brown shell is no problem for squirrels. But you will need a nutcracker to eat the tasty nut inside.

Sticks and twists, knots and rings, crunchy brown pretzels come in many shapes and sizes.

9

Brown for Breakfast

They're known as pancakes,
flapjacks, or even griddle cakes.
But whatever you call them,
everyone likes them cooked
to a golden brown.

Popping and sizzling sounds come from the kitchen. Crispy, brown bacon is frying in a pan. Breakfast is almost ready.

Cinnamon buns are sticky and sweet. Their curls and swirls are filled with spicy brown cinnamon.

Mealtime Brown

When it comes to bread, brown is the best. A sandwich with whole wheat bread makes a healthy meal.

Turkey drumsticks
have a built-in handle.
Grab on and gobble up
this tasty brown meat.

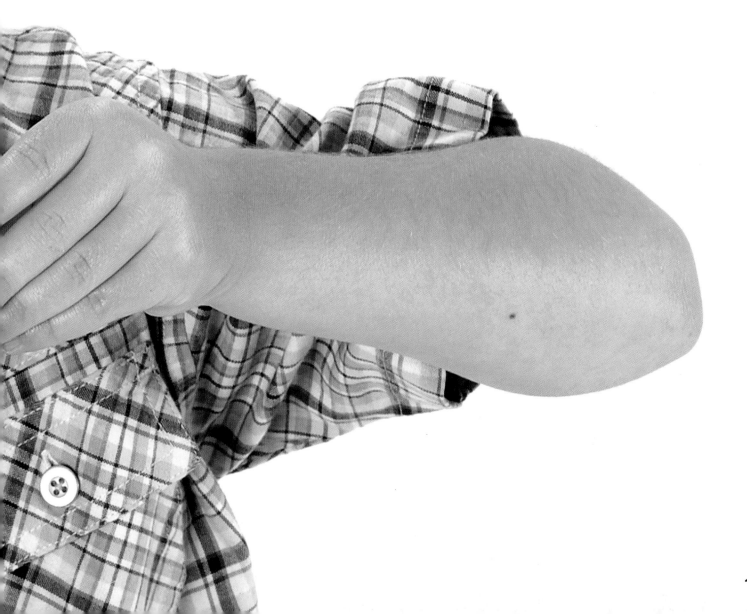

Ooops! Who spilled the beans? It's no secret that baked beans are made with brown sugar, molasses, and tasty spices.

Brown So Sweet

Mmmmm! Smooth brown peanut butter tastes good all by itself. Team it with chocolate, and you've got a really sweet treat!

23

Dots on fudge, what are those? They look like tasty dominoes. Creamy fudge is so sweet that just a little is enough to eat.

A batch of brown gingerbread men smell as good as they taste. What other brown foods make you smile?

Pancake Taco

Sweeten up your morning with this twist on the taco.

What You Will Need

Pancakes

Coconut shavings

Kiwifruit

Strawberries

Chocolate chips

Red and yellow food coloring

Whipped cream (optional)

How to Make a Pancake Taco

1. Ask an adult to make a stack of pancakes. Set aside. The cooled pancakes will be the taco shells.

2. Place a handful of coconut shavings in a small bowl. Stir in a drop of red and yellow food coloring. The coconut shavings should turn orange like cheese.

3. Have an adult help slice the strawberries and kiwifruit. These items will look like tomatoes and lettuce for your pancake taco.

4. To build the taco, grab a cooled pancake. Sprinkle on a few chocolate chips.

5. Next add kiwifruit and strawberries.

6. Sprinkle colored coconut shavings on top.

7. For an extra treat, add a squirt of whipped cream (it will look like sour cream).

8. Eat and enjoy!

Glossary

cinnamon (SIN-uh-muhn)—a spice that comes from the inner bark of a tropical tree

domino (DOM-uh-noh)—a small rectangular tile divided into two halves that are blank or contain dots; people use domino tiles to play a game called dominoes.

drumstick (DRUHM-stik)—the leg portion of a turkey

flapjack (FLAP-jak)—another name for a pancake

gingerbread (JIN-jur-bred)—a cake or cookie flavored with ginger and other spices

griddle cake (GRID-uhl KAYK)—another name for a pancake

molasses (muh-LASS-iz)—thick, sweet syrup made when sugarcane is turned into syrup

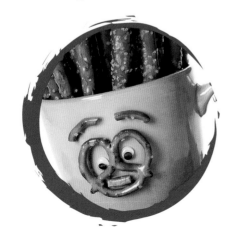

Read More

Dahl, Michael. *Brown: Seeing Brown All Around Us.* Colors. Mankato, Minn.: Capstone Press, 2005.

Whitehouse, Patricia. *Brown Foods.* The Colors We Eat. Chicago: Heinemann, 2004.

Internet Sites

FactHound offers a safe, fun way to find Internet sites related to this book. All of the sites on FactHound have been researched by our staff.

Here's how:

1. Visit *www.facthound.com*

2. Type in this special code 0736853804 for age-appropriate sites. Or enter a search word related to this book for a more general search.

3. Click on the Fetch It button.

FactHound will fetch the best sites for you!

Index